# FINDING **JOY** IN RETIREMENT

*4 steps to discover meaning in life after work*

**JON GLASS PhD & DAVID KENNEDY**

First published in 2019 by Grammar Factory Pty Ltd

© Jon Glass & David Kennedy 2019

The moral rights of the authors have been asserted

All rights reserved. Except as permitted under the *Australian Copyright Act 1968* (for example, a fair dealing for the purposes of study, research, criticism or review), no part of this book may be reproduced, stored in a retrieval system, communicated or transmitted in any form or by any means without prior written permission.

All enquiries should be made to the authors.

National Library of Australia Cataloguing-in-Publication entry:

| | |
|---|---|
| Creators: | Glass, Jon. 1952– author |
| | Kennedy David J. 1978– author. |
| Title: | Finding Joy in Retirement / Jon Glass & David Kennedy. |
| ISBN: | 978-0-6484307-9-7 (paperback) |
| | 978-0-6485850-0-8 (ebook) |
| Subjects: | Retirement–Australia–Planning. |
| | Ageing–Australia. |
| | Retirement age–Australia. |
| | Older people–Australia. |
| | Coaching |

Printed in Australia by McPhersons Printing
Cover design by Designerbility
Book production by Grammar Factory
Editorial by Jem Bates Editing Services

*'The powerful play goes on, and you may contribute a verse.'*

**WALT WHITMAN**

*Gratitude and thanks go to Marg and Kate.*

# TABLE OF CONTENTS

| | |
|---|---|
| Preface: An unlikely partnership | 9 |
| Introduction | 13 |
| The case for a conversation with a retirement coach | 19 |
| **MISSING:** What aspects of your working life will you miss and how will you replace them? | 27 |
| **MEASURING:** How busy are you, and how busy do you want to be? | 45 |
| **MEANING:** What is your purpose in life from here? | 57 |
| **MASTERY:** What are your goals in retirement and how will you move purposefully towards them? | 75 |
| **REAL PEOPLE, REAL STORIES:** Learning from tales of retirement transition | 87 |
| Conclusion | 113 |
| About the authors | 117 |
| Hear from Jon's retirement coaching clients | 123 |
| Sources | 125 |

# PREFACE:
# AN UNLIKELY PARTNERSHIP

Here we are, two finance guys teaming up to write a book on retirement that has nothing to do with money. How did that happen? In simple terms, we have a shared passion for helping people from all walks of life to make an effective emotional transition to retirement – an enthusiasm inspired by our different backgrounds, as we describe in 'About the authors' at the back.

Why do we still divide the world into old and young people, workers and retirees, productive and useless? Imagine a world where ageing was viewed positively, where older people were revered, and where growing old was seen as an opportunity to tap into your true purpose for the benefit of yourself, your family and the community.

Yet the very language of retirement brings to the fore negative ideas of leaving something behind, without a sense of a clear destination. It has the connotation of a person having outlasted their usefulness, when in truth there are many ways to contribute to society by making productive use of your time after you have stopped work.

As many have observed before, we tend to hear far more of the negative phrase 'retire from' than of the more positive 'retire to'. Most of us know someone who has struggled mentally and emotionally soon after clocking off for the last time. When your purpose, routine and social network are heavily dependent on your career, the transition from employee to retiree is fraught with danger.

In a March 2019 interview with Emma Plumb of *Respectful Exits,* American author Chip Conley neatly captures this dilemma. 'Our current process of retirement,' he argues, 'doesn't serve either the company or the older employee. To be a 100% employee on a Friday and a 100% retiree (0% employee) on Monday is cruel and unusual punishment and may accelerate poor health conditions since so much of our social life comes from the workplace.'

It is easy to forget that the idea of retirement at age sixty-five really only came about in Australia in the early 1900s when the Age Pension was introduced. At the time, only a very small percentage of the population lived into their seventies and eighties, so planning for this phase of life was not a high priority. Statistically, you were lucky to make it to sixty-five, and any time beyond that was a bonus.

But over the past century or so, we have added more than twenty-five years to our average life expectancy, a gift bestowed upon us by medical and technological advances and rising standards of living. These days people in their sixties are healthier, and live longer, than at any point in history, and the challenge they face is how to make the most of all those extra years.

The less thought you have given to who you will be, how you will structure your days and the activities you will engage in beyond the workplace, the higher the probability that you will find yourself 'stuck' between your old identity and an unwritten future of possibilities in retirement.

We liken the retirement transition to walking over a bridge, connecting one phase of your life to another. By preparing consciously, you increase your chances of a successful crossing.

In 2017 the Australian Bureau of Statistics found that of those retirees who recently returned to the workforce, nearly one-third did so simply out of 'boredom' and because they 'needed something to do'. Why do so many people walk blindfolded towards retirement, and is there a better way to prepare?

We believe the answer is an unequivocal 'yes', and the aim of this book is to show you how.

**JON AND DAVID**

# INTRODUCTION

Some books are written to entertain (think of novels) while others are written to educate (think of textbooks). Perhaps you'll choose to read this book from cover to cover in one sitting; more likely you'll dip into sections that catch your eye and offer a new perspective. At the very least, we hope your copy becomes recognisable only by its coffee stains, dog-eared pages and illegible notes in the margins.

Our aim is to share the ideas, tools and conversations on which Jon has built his retirement coaching practice, 64 PLUS, in order to shift your thinking and open your eyes to the infinite possibilities of life after work. David then provides a window into the priceless experiences of others, with real stories that shed light on the common obstacles to making a successful retirement transition, while inspiring you to plan for, and work towards, the life that YOU wish to lead beyond the nine to five.

During the course of your career, you didn't turn up each day hoping for the best, letting fate decide the course of your working life. Quite the opposite — you planned, strived, struggled, reflected, changed course and worked purposefully towards your goals.

Think about how you have made other big decisions in your life:

- Did you buy your first house simply because you saw a nice photograph of the front fence?
- Did you get married on a reality TV show?
- Did you change careers based on someone's mere suggestion at a party?

Chances are, prior to committing to any of these milestones in life, you planned and prepared far more thoroughly to ensure you were set up for success. Yet, even though many of us will spend decades in retirement, the time and effort put into preparing consciously for this phase of life is sadly lacking. We propose that those who fail to purposefully design their life after work risk reaching year five in retirement only to lament that they simply didn't know five years ago what they know now.

Conscious preparation matters, because time is precious, and there are few more hollow feelings than the realisation that you have wasted the early years of retirement through complacency and lack of planning. Imagine travelling to some exotic overseas location. There, being shown around by a guide with 'local knowledge' can make the difference between an ordinary holiday and a life-changing experience. When visiting a new place for the first time (such as retirement), there is real value in enlisting a guide to show you around.

It is natural to feel anxious about confronting a life beyond work. While clichéd portrayals abound of retirement as an endless summer of beach walks, golf and overseas travel, the reality rarely lives up to the marketing. The glossy brochures would have us believe that retirement is about sailing off into the sunset, but the truth is you are heading into uncharted waters.

There is a clear parallel between retirement coaching and financial planning - they are two sides of the same coin, although this is not widely understood today.

Let's go into a little more detail. What do they have in common? In simple terms, the long-term process of financial planning involves pursuing a savings strategy that will allow you to replace your regular salary with ongoing income from your investments when you stop working. Done well, such planning provides financial peace of mind when you no longer receive a regular pay cheque.

Yet, if we accept the old adage that 'money can't buy happiness', then you do yourself a disservice by preparing for retirement by addressing only your financial needs. While extremely common, this approach neglects the need to prepare financially *and* emotionally for life after work. This leads to our central idea, which we explain below.

While there are probably elements of work you will be glad to leave behind, let's consider some of the things your job (or business) provides that you may miss when you retire:

| | |
|---|---|
| **MEANING & PURPOSE** | You could easily define your purpose as a worker |
| **ROUTINE** | You knew where you would be every Monday at 9am |
| **IDENTITY** | You had a job title and you felt you were needed |
| **ACHIEVEMENT** | You finished a successful project and felt good |
| **SOCIAL CONNECTION** | You had work colleagues you could relate to |
| **VALIDATION** | Your boss told you how good you were (sometimes) |
| **SATISFACTION & PLEASURE** | You completed a week of work and sat back and smiled |

We are all different, but to varying degrees, each of these elements contribute to our mental and emotional wellbeing. When you retire, your meaning and purpose in life may be less clear, you may feel uncertain of your identity, or you may find that opportunities for social interaction are less plentiful.

We believe that by acknowledging these realities, and consciously planning ahead, rather than spending those precious early years going around in circles, you are more likely to enjoy an easier and more fulfilling path to retirement. That is our hope for you.

# THE CASE FOR A CONVERSATION WITH A RETIREMENT COACH

*'Like a lot of new retirees, I thought I had things organised.
But I was thinking financially, not psychologically.
It turned out, as I'm sure it does for a lot of men,
that I was totally unprepared for the psychological changes
brought about by retirement.' (David)*

The essence of retirement coaching is to guide the client towards finding meaning and purpose in his or her post-work life. This can be a challenging task without some sort of outside help. Assuming you already have a plan in place to address your financial needs, engaging the services of a retirement coach will ensure you have a lifestyle plan that addresses your emotional needs.

## What is retirement coaching?

Retirement coaches commonly work with people who are approaching retirement or recently retired. The role of the coach in working with their clients is to explore some of the big questions that will confront them when they decide to transition to life beyond their career. For example: What is truly important to them? How would they like the next phase of their life to unfold? What goals and objectives matter to them and their family?

Among people close to retirement, it is common to hear these remarks:

- 'I have no idea what I'll do — I'll think about it when the time comes.'
- 'I can't leave work yet because there's no one who can take over my job if I leave.'
- 'Work stimulates me and provides me with friends.'

Among retired people, it is more common to hear these sorts of remarks:

- 'I really need to get out more.'
- 'I suffer from relevance deprivation syndrome — I used to be needed, in demand.'
- 'I am a slave to my free time.'

The questions coaches ask are designed to encourage pre-retirees to think deeply about their identity before and after retirement, and, importantly, how they might structure their life in retirement in order to fill the void often left when full-time work ceases. For example: As the author of your own retirement script, what will you write? How different will it look from your working life? Will you create a more authentic balance in your life than you have been able to achieve in the past? Will you have more time for family and friends, hobbies and interests? What is truly important to you in the next chapter of your life, and what planning is needed in order to tick all those items off your bucket list, now that you have the time to do so?

While there is a methodology behind every coaching interaction, no two client conversations are the same. For example, the coach may pick up on a theme to develop further — let's say the level of busyness or idleness in the client's daily life since retirement. But here's the point. The client can and probably will discuss this with reference to examples and feelings across time, comparing today with, say, twenty years ago — all in the same conversation. There will also be other dynamics at play in this conversation.

Building on these ideas, the coach will seek opportunities to work on the client's narrative. Clarification may be important; reformulation can also be very useful — both of them in pursuit of a deeper *joint* understanding of the client's situation. There is no set formula. What there must be is good listening, reflection and observation of the client's tone, words and body language.

## How is retirement coaching different to other forms of professional advice?

A recent study published by Forbes found that, on average, a patient visiting their GP will be listened to for just eleven seconds before being interrupted. In a retirement coaching session, by contrast, it is typical for a client to speak for the majority of the allotted time, while the coach guides the conversation with questions and reflection.

The coaching session is a great opportunity to be listened to and to work through important issues. A retirement coach offers you the chance to formulate your feelings and thoughts about retirement, without any pressure to arrive at a set resolution. Everyone deserves to be heard and listened to fully and attentively. How often does that opportunity present itself in life?

But, of course, to hear and to listen are not quite the same thing, as was captured beautifully by Oscar Wilde in the opening lines of *The Importance of Being Earnest*, in which Algernon gets up from the piano to address his butler, Lane:

**Algernon:** Did you hear what I was playing, Lane?

**Lane:** I didn't think it polite to listen, sir.

# STRANGERS ON A TRAIN

Imagine overhearing a conversation on a train that goes like this:

It's soon evident that one of the two speakers (we'll call them Mike and Jim) is about to retire while the other retired three years ago.

Mike: So what will you do with yourself when you retire, Jim?

Jim: Relax, travel a bit, play golf, relax.

Mike: Interesting, but say a year on?

Jim: We'll see. You've been retired for, what, around three years now, Mike? Don't you miss work?

Mike: I did at first. Actually, the transition from work to retirement was stressful and difficult in a way I didn't expect. My job gave me a clear purpose. Also, I missed the friendships. But now I've made new friends and I see them all the time.

Jim: How did you do that?

Mike: I realised early on that I really wanted to do voluntary work. There's plenty around, and you meet new people and test yourself in new situations. It's not like work at all. And you make friends there.

Jim: Do you do that five days a week?

Mike: Oh no. I'm also studying Japanese. Seriously. It's an open-ended commitment. I can do it at any time of the day for as long as I am motivated. Then, when I go to Japan next month, I will have a much better chance to understand their culture than when you and I went on that work trip ten years ago. Do you remember?

Jim: Yes, I remember that – it all seemed pretty strange. But I think I'll actually miss the pressure of work. It really motivates me.

Mike: I make my own pressure. No boss tells me what to do. Except for the voluntary work, which I can turn off when I want to, I am my own boss.

Jim: How did you work through all these issues?

Mike: I got help. From a retirement coach. He's not a financial planner but he listens. He helped me to find my meaning and purpose after I stopped work. I can give you his details, if you like.

In the next section of the book, we will take you through the ideas and concepts as experienced by Jon's clients in his retirement coaching practice, 64 PLUS. Clients are coached individually over several specifically designed sessions using the '4M Process', which starts with the following simple yet powerful questions - from the framework of either contemplation of retirement or being newly retired:

- **MISSING** — What aspects of your working life will you miss and how will you replace them?

- **MEASURING** — How busy are you and how busy do you want to be?

- **MEANING** — What is your purpose in life from here?

- **MASTERY** — What are your goals in retirement, and how will you move purposefully towards them?

# MISSING:
# WHAT ASPECTS OF YOUR WORKING LIFE WILL YOU MISS AND HOW WILL YOU REPLACE THEM?

*'It's an exploration stage in life. I think you've got your basic interests that you've always had, and then there are the new activities that come up by surprise.' (Robyn)*

You spend a very large proportion of your life in the workplace — perhaps in a single occupation, perhaps in many jobs. Will you miss aspects of your working life when you retire?

## Overcoming retirement fears and creating your own order

Let's explore the transition from work to post-work in order to understand it better.

As an analogue of your working life, imagine a fortress. Inside the fortress there are people and jobs, order and method, activity and purpose. When you stand on the battlements and look out beyond your fields towards the horizon, you have an impression of disorder. This is how you may think about life after work. As you come to the end of your working life, you may imagine post-work as a scary place, a bit like the wilderness beyond the controlled order of your lands and castle.

The retirement coach's purpose is to help you to see that those fears have no foundation, that once you have stopped working you can shape your own destiny while maintaining the level of control you feel you need.

Does this sound familiar? A good financial planner also aims to control the fears and uncertainties you have around the substitution of a regular pay cheque with a pension. Both advisers are life guides.

Of course, countless others have travelled out into the world beyond the fortress before you and, with or without a coach's support, have found meaning in their lives. You need not be lost in the wilderness, for there are some well-defined paths through this landscape that you can follow.

## What is your reason for being?

The Japanese word *ikigai* broadly translates as 'reason for being' or 'your motivation for getting out of bed in the morning'. Let's divide life into four phases – childhood, young adult, worker and retired person.

If a child doesn't want to get out of bed in the morning to get ready for school, there will almost certainly be a parent who 'facilitates' the process. A young adult will likely have a stronger motivation to get started in the morning, though this may not be sufficient to do the job every day. Once in the workforce, no matter what your level of enthusiasm to face the day, how many employers will tolerate regular, unexplained absences?

Finally, in the post-work phase, it gets interesting. What is your motivation to get out of bed? What is your purpose? What are the sources of meaning in your life?

## The power of structure and certainty

There are many differences between the working and post-work worlds. Two words that frequently come up in discussions with coaching clients are 'certainty' and 'structure'.

Put simply, work offers certainty of both purpose and objectives, and a structured timetable to adhere to in order to achieve those objectives. After you stop working, any structures will be largely self-imposed — think of routines around household chores, grandchildren, charity work, pursuit of a hobby or exercise.

But perhaps you have always longed to escape from rigid structures, which you associate with your working life, in which case you will need to learn to live with a lack of certainty. That's not necessarily a bad thing; lack of certainty can be quite liberating and lead to unforeseen opportunities.

There is no right or wrong here. However, it is useful to acknowledge these different possibilities; to do so can save a lot of wasted time and energy on challenges that can be readily resolved — with or without the help of a retirement coach.

During that initial flush of freedom around retirement, there is unlikely to be any great urgency. You can start by enjoying the sense of release from the rigid routine of work. It may feel strange at first; after all, it's something you have never experienced before.

Without forcing it, over time you will likely develop some ideas about the structure you want to establish in your post-work life. This will centre on activities or plans that have *unique meaning for you*, not someone else.

Build that structure, like a house, and celebrate the construction of each room, as each starts to add some level of certainty in your life. Champagne corks everywhere. The bigger the structure, the less the uncertainty.

You can end this process whenever you choose. It's your house, so you can build it to the size that suits you. And remember: It's not a permanent structure — you can renovate or rebuild whenever you wish to.

## Who am I?

Do you remember the parlour game 'Who am I', where you are given clues and have to guess the person's identity? You might be told, for example, that 'in 1492 he sailed the ocean blue', at which stage you will either blurt out 'Columbus' or ask for a further clue, such as his nationality. And so on.

If a younger you were the subject in this game, the first clue might state the work you do. 'He is a salesman.' Need more clues? Okay: 'He is over the age of 30.' And so on.

If you are the subject in the game after retirement, though, it will immediately become apparent that something is missing. What could be the first clue? Yes, you may be a parent, a son, a daughter, a grandparent — but what do you *do*? How do you define your role in the world? Who *are* you now?

This is one of the key challenges of retirement.

## INSIGHTS FROM SOMEONE WHO RECENTLY STOPPED WORKING

This wide-ranging conversation produced some interesting ideas about the feelings experienced when work stops — some of them looking back, most of them looking forward.

Although the worker has retired, the world of work continues for others. It is this that can generate Relevance Deficit

Syndrome (RDS) in the retiree. As the conversation progressed, several thoughts along these lines emerged:

- People used to seek out my thoughts, opinions and guidance.
- I miss things that work provided, including the income.
- How can I contribute to society now that I have stopped working?

Certain of my habits were suppressed by my working life, such as sleeping in, watching daytime TV, doing nothing. Sure, they were mostly inappropriate during my working life, especially Monday through Friday, but now I can be kinder to myself. Why not grant myself permission to indulge in these practices occasionally?

Now, this person happened to have a working partner, rather than one who was always at home. So the old maxim 'I married you for breakfast and dinner but definitely not for lunch' doesn't apply. Not yet anyway. But there is the challenge ahead of how they can enjoy end-of-day conversations together once they no longer both work. It's a challenge worth rising to, especially given that the working partner is likely to be heavily engaged in work projects and, as we know, that can be quite a dominant theme in dinnertime conversations.

## Three myths of retirement

What is retirement, and how does it feel to be retired? Before you go through the process yourself, you can either observe and talk to all the retired people you know or meet, or not think about it much at all. Either way, you will likely be hostage to some foundational myths about retirement. Here are three:

- *Retirement is defined by how much money you have.* Well, yes, it is probably good to have more money than less, but it turns out that the emotional aspects of retirement can be more significant than the financial.

- *Retirement is the phase of life when everything becomes easy.* How 'easy' might be defined will be very personal and individual, but the truth is that all stages of life present problems to be solved.

- *Retirement represents the dead end of life.* Reject that. It's as lively, challenging and exciting as you want to make it.

Exploring some of these myths more deeply will move you closer to an understanding of what you can make of your own retirement.

## The retirement transition

Retirement may look like it is a clear-cut event at a single point in time, but it is commonly experienced as a transition that unfolds over months or even years.

*Transition* is an interesting word. In its abstract sense it denotes movement, though in an almost cold, mechanical way. But it also relates to the word *passage*, which has warmer, more human associations to movement.

In relation to retirement, we will concentrate narrowly on the emotional engagement a retiree has with self, family, friends, work and any of a number of other agents with whom he or she negotiates during the transition.

For example, it may take time to process that, after not dressing up for work each weekday morning as you have done for so long, you will have a lot of time on your hands and a lot of space in your home. Both new circumstances need to be negotiated.

In this transition you may find yourself in one or several of these states of mind:

- Looking back and missing what you once had in your job.
- Passing almost seamlessly into a happy retirement life.
- Going through some kind of torturous passage towards the unknown.
- Developing goals that define your activities in retirement.

Creating goals isn't going to suit everyone. Some personality types are goal-driven; others are happy to take it as it comes. You may recognise which category you fall into through reflecting on your habits at work. There is no right answer here.

Transition to retirement is not an easy emotional concept to grasp but, done well, it is your passage to the green pastures of a new life.

## How does it feel?

For some people retirement entails an abrupt shift from work to non-work, while for others it's a gradual shift via the pathway of part-time work.

This transition towards full retirement generates a range of feelings that can be unsettling. Here are some common symptoms:

- You are losing track of time, deadlines having become less part of your daily routine.
- You no longer need to find free time, as it is 'everywhere' in your life.
- You *feel* 'retired', however, you don't really understand that term.
- You talk less about 'we' when discussing your interactions with colleagues at work.

You may wish to reflect on some or all of these.

# New beginnings

Suppose you have just retired or are about to do so, and you want to try out some new things in your life. Are there activities that you have neglected through lack of time or opportunity, or things you want to try for the first time?

What will give you the confidence to even start? It's a question Goethe, the great German writer, was all over. He said, at least in English translation and quoted freely:

*'The moment one definitely commits oneself, then ... all sorts of things occur to help one that would never otherwise have occurred. Boldness has genius, power, and magic in it. Begin it now.'*

Why not commit to a new path and see how the universe surprises you and comes to your aid?

## The path to retirement and sports coaches

Imagine a fridge door with this thought-generating note stuck on it, placed there by someone who is about to retire from a lifetime of work.

- Enough money?
- Play golf.
- Garden.
- Go on a cruise.
- Grandkids.

It makes sense that the first item tops the list. It points towards financial planning, and there is an abundance of choice when seeking help there; it's possible most retirees seek some form of financial advice. But the other items on the list are different. Why?

They are different because they are very personal, and people tend to have very different emotional needs. So the list is a good place to start, but the next step is to begin to ponder and reflect on *your* list. Here are some ideas that are worth reflecting on as you do that:

- Work was a place to go outside of the home that offered you a shared space, an office perhaps, a familiar building or environment.
- At work you had tasks to complete, deadlines to meet, people to work with — some pleasant, some perhaps less so.
- Work dictated how you used time for a large part of your life and, therefore, restricted your personal choices, which wasn't always a bad thing.
- Work gave you things to think about and talk about, to complain about and rejoice in, with family and friends.

On retirement, all of the above simply evaporate into thin air. You may be asking yourself what you have lost, and what you can look forward to. You may equally appreciate what you are glad to be rid of, but also what you are unsure about in the next phase of your life. These are big questions, on which the external perspective of a coach can be very helpful.

Let's discuss sports coaches. We all know the valuable role they play, whether in team sports such as football, basketball and cricket, or for individual competitors such as tennis players. What does this have to do with retirement coaching?

There are distinct similarities between these coaching disciplines. Both focus on motivation and the prospect of improvement where you obtain an independent view in order to help solve a problem.

## EVEN CHAMPIONS NEED A COACH

*'The written word is no substitute for a wise, resourceful coach.'*

**HERB ELLIOTT**

Speak to most athletes and you will learn that the benefit of a good coach is less about honing technique, and more about encouraging the right mindset, sharpening your focus and building your self-belief.

An external perspective matters. Effective coaches open your eyes to new ways of thinking that have the potential to build character, transform behaviour and improve results.

When Olympic gold medallist and world champion athlete Herb Elliott first met Percy Cerutty, he knew little of the eccentric running coach who would go on to shape his philosophy on life and extraordinary career.

According to Australian Olympic Committee historian Harry Gordon, Elliott was unbeaten in forty-two events over 1,500 metres and a mile between 1957 and 1961. So dominant was he that his world record time in the 1,500 metres at the 1960 Rome Olympics, where he won the gold medal by twenty metres, would have been fast enough to win the same event at the Seoul (1988), Barcelona (1992) and Atlanta Olympics (1996) decades later.

Of Elliott's coach, Gordon says, 'Cerutty was an eccentric visionary who worked on the bodies and minds of his charges. The challenge he offered Elliott was not to beat opponents, but to conquer himself.'

A few years earlier, Cerutty had travelled to Aquinas College in Perth to give a series of talks. Elliott was seventeen years old and, unbeknownst to him, his father had invited Cerutty to the family home for lunch.

One of the keys to Cerutty's impact as a coach was his ability to ask the right questions. During a long conversation on athletics, he would play devil's advocate by questioning why young Elliott would want to run around in circles, always ending up back where he started.

'What you want to do is utterly trivial,' Percy said. 'Why would you want to give up your life for that?'

Elliott didn't have a logical answer, but the conversation that followed would remain with him for a lifetime.

'Your sport is going to give you the opportunity to grow into a greater, stronger, better human being. If you're going to do it to the very best of your ability, you're going to be out of your comfort zone all the time. And human beings only ever grow when they're outside their comfort zone,' Percy said.

In a 2008 interview with Ian Jobling for the Sport Oral History Project, Elliott said, 'I didn't realise the significance of what he said and what a big part it would play in my life at the time. On reflection, looking back on it, it was a very significant moment ... In those days a good coach was perceived as a person with a big mouth that spent all their time shouting at you ... Percy was never like that. His modus operandi was not threats — it wasn't bullying. It was philosophically, mentally and spiritually challenging you. And then just letting you go.'

An advocate of re-invention, Cerutty's uniqueness was his ability to influence the mental development of his athletes, and offer new ways of thinking to give them an edge that was near impossible to replicate.

> Elliott says, 'Percy helped me by releasing in my mind and soul a power that I only vaguely thought existed.'
>
> Of course, coaching relationships go far beyond the world of sport. Entertainers employ voice coaches, a tutor helps a high school student improve their results, while someone approaching retirement may engage a retirement coach to help them prepare effectively for life after work.
>
> Cerutty captured his unconventional philosophies on life and achievement in a series of books. On the link between emotions and outcomes, he said, 'to become great, whether an artist, a writer, a philosopher or creator or scientist, even as one great in sport, the secret lies, assuming there is some native ability in the first place, in one factor above all others — emotion.'

## Centres of retirement

In psychology there is a useful concept called *locus of control*. It helps to explain the extent to which a person feels they have control over their life. Your locus of control remains important throughout your life, including in retirement.

At retirement several things happen. Work ceases to be the centre of your existence. Family, in the traditional sense, may also have ceased to be central simply as a function of age — to put it bluntly, the kids have left home.

The question is what to do about this loss of activities that were hitherto at the centre of your life. Nature abhors a vacuum, so this hole will have to be filled. Not everyone will recognise this clearly and objectively. Some will understand and respond to the new circumstances; others will be warned but will ignore the facts, though they may bubble away subconsciously.

In practical terms, you may look to substitute the central activities of work and family with, say, directors' positions or grandparental activities. Some, however, conceive of such responses as being like a shipwrecked sailor clinging to a sinking ship in mid ocean. They are convinced of the need to move away from the old centre and find other ways to fill the vacuum.

## Wexit: What happens when you decide to leave work?

A few years ago, Greece was a possible candidate for being the first country to leave the European Union. It didn't happen then; it may or may not happen in the future. At the time, the world's press fell in love with the term 'Grexit', as it described the prospect succinctly and was a boon for headline writers. And of course we are all familiar with the more recent drama surrounding 'Brexit'.

We want to propose a new word to substitute for the emotionally charged language of 'retirement': Meet Wexit, or work exit.

Just likes its etymological cousins (Grexit and Brexit), Wexit demands answers to certain important questions such as what, why, when and how, though it's unlikely to stir up the same kind of public protest and political controversy. No foreign ministers, trade delegations, lawyers or prime ministers in the spotlight; instead there will be employers, colleagues, superannuation consultants — oh, and don't forget family and friends.

But there is much more at stake than the Wexit itself. That may turn out to be quite simple: employed one day, out of work the next. What really counts is what happens next. So Wexit is really the first part of a longer, more significant process in which you work out and plan the next thirty or so years of your life.

## Monday morning blues

Do you feel like singing this blues song?

*I woke up this morning
To see my work has gone.*

Imagine this common scenario: You retired on Friday, and on Monday morning you turn to your partner and ask expectantly, 'So what are we doing today?' To which he or she replies, 'I don't know what you're doing but I have plans for the day. See you at dinner.'

On the threshold of retirement, there are three main strategic directions you can take:

- You can treat this phase of life as a journey without a clear destination. The danger with this approach is that you may spend valuable years in search of that destination.

- You can talk to other people who have gone through the experience themselves. The problem here is that they will be talking about *their* experience, not yours.

- You can find a good retirement coach who can guide you towards formulating the questions to ask yourself and then help you to extract your own answers.

**REFLECTION ACTIVITIES**

- Talk to people about some of the common myths of retirement.

- Can you have a successful sports team without a coach? Can you have a happy retirement without a coach?

- What is your *ikigai*, or reason to get out of bed each day?

# MEASURING: HOW BUSY ARE YOU, AND HOW BUSY DO YOU WANT TO BE?

*'I actually need a routine, and I have to have a timetable. I don't know whether it's because I am very institutionalised, but I like to have some anchors around which I can then build other activities.' (Catherine)*

When you were at work, wasn't there a whole lot happening each day? An interesting aspect of retirement is noticing how empty your diary might be. How would you react to that: positively, negatively or not at all?

## Time in retirement

After retirement, a funny thing happens with time and how you feel about it. It's as if time stretches. What does this mean?

Time is a strange thing. Unlike vision and sound, which we perceive directly through eyes and ears, we can't directly perceive time; we simply notice things around us, things from which our brain creates a time sequence.

If you are doing a boring job that prompts you to glance at your watch or iPhone every few minutes, then you are measuring time in one way. If you are playing tennis with such joy and focus that you notice the time only when the next players stake their claim to the court, then that is quite another measure. In the first case, time passes so slowly it's as though each hour is twice as long; in the second, time races by at what seems like twice its 'normal' speed.

Time is the way we record, think about and are struck by the movement of the events of life around us. Alternatively, it is a trace of our memories. So time is a very personal deduction from experience. We think of the clock as a definitive, universal measure of time, but it's not that simple. Our language offers any number of examples of the subjective experience of time: 'I lost track of time'; 'Time weighed heavily on me'; 'I have time to kill'; 'Time flies, doesn't it?'

All this means you can feel surprisingly busy with your postwork activities even though, compared with your daily fulltime work schedule, your diary may now look relatively bare. No more back-to-back meetings. It's your choice as to how you fill your day, but there is one important consideration. That is to seek out activities that have *meaning* for you.

When you worked, you would jealously protect your 'spare time'. Much of it would be allocated to shopping, transporting children to various sporting locations, cooking, laundry and other household chores as well as to leisure pursuits. But what exactly is the meaning of spare time in the post-work world? There is no simple answer to this question. In retirement you will have the time to think about these things.

So to finish, some tips:

- Be flexible, and try out many things.
- Build new networks of friends.
- Be bored, sometimes.
- Beware of daytime TV.

## The O'clock syndrome

What is the O'clock syndrome? It's the imperative, the must-do, that looms over the world of work when you are a full-time worker. Every hour, possibly every half hour, there's a meeting, an appointment, a deadline. You know the feeling: You dash off an email or two, flick through a document, give someone a quick call, and before you know it you are in the swim of that O'clock obligation. This is probably the daily rhythm of your working life, particularly if you work in an office.

Retirement presents a different face of time. You have a chance to set your own daily and weekly rhythm, and choose the projects you engage in rather than forever responding to the piecemeal demands of others. Now you can take control of your time, setting aside an activity to go for a walk, cook a meal, read a book, watch TV, relax. The choice of activities is yours to make. Experiment and see what works for you, and change activities anytime that suits you, without asking permission.

Where once the weekend was keenly anticipated as a reward for the stresses of the Monday-to-Friday working week, after retirement the weekend's halo has slipped, its special distinction in danger of becoming irrelevant.

Weekends were easy to define; at the end of the working week, they offered an opportunity for rest and recreation. The weekend was your lifeboat to sanity, a chance to do whatever you wanted to do, or had to do, but had no time for during the week. Above all, it was a chance to de-stress. After retirement, the weekend becomes just like any other part of the week.

Or does it? For while it may mean less to you directly, for those still working, who are all around you, it remains special, and you cannot but be aware of this. Perhaps that is all a weekend needs to mean to a retired person. It is what others around you celebrate. Meantime, you set your own routine.

In retirement, full or partial, the phone rings less often, email traffic is less urgent and the bustle of people around you diminishes, unless you choose otherwise. Home becomes more important because you are spending more time there than you used to. Now you have more control over the flow of your activities, and are less a prisoner of the passing hours. The O'clock syndrome gives way to what we call *the sundial in the lounge room*.

## Energy in retirement

There is a connection between energy and retirement. Instead of constructing the day according to the clock — tick tock, another meeting, stress, stress — consider basing it on how you expend energy. As a model, think of the electricity grid: You draw from it for your energy needs or contribute to it from the power collected by your solar panels.

How will you allocate the energy of your day? You will likely have periods of intense energy expenditure on a task, periods of restful activities during which you recharge, and other times that are more or less energy neutral. Now the clock is no longer your master, the day has a completely different flavour. Using energy as a framing mechanism brings you closer to dividing the day into things you love doing and those that are a pain to you. Isn't this approach likely to reduce your stress in retirement?

## The space of retirement

'Space: the final frontier,' intones the voiceover on the TV show *Star Trek*. The act of retirement has many aspects, some constant and predictable, some variable and ever changing. The home is a constant. Or is it?

Let's look at an example. In this long-standing couple, he has already retired and she is about to retire. The status quo sees her out of the house from breakfast to dinner each day, Monday to Friday. Their weekend routine involves many joint activities.

Once she retires, the house becomes a shared space seven days a week. That's equivalent to another 2.5 weekends in that space every week. This is where it gets complicated.

Where once they spent only weekends and evenings together in the house, now — and for the next thirty or so years — they will both share the space all day, every day. This will create challenges. For example, how might the house be divided into 'public' and 'private' spaces for each of them? And what will each contribute in terms of ideas, activities to enjoy and conversations to share, which may include opportunities to discuss and resolve problems in their relationship?

These questions may provoke interesting and animated debates around how much time they should spend together and how much time they should spend pursuing independent lives.

There is no formula here. This is a time for them to be flexible, to talk openly, to experiment, to make mistakes and learn from them, 'to boldly go' (in the language of *Star Trek*) where they haven't been before.

Let's conclude by talking about the related concept of the empty nest, or how it feels to be a parent whose children have grown up and left home. This profound change can be a difficult transition for parents, prompting a sense of sadness and loss, just as retirement can trigger a sense of loss of meaning.

At the same time, empty nesters can enjoy many benefits:

- With fewer dependents, financial pressures ease.
- The house is suddenly tidier and less chaotic — even before the Marie Kondo moment.
- The disappearance of food from the refrigerator is back under control.
- The car belongs to its owners.

Are these benefits enough to outweigh the negatives? How do you reconcile these two opposite feelings: missing your children every day, while engaging positively with the changes caused by their moving on?

## Measurement matters

In the world of work, productivity really matters. 'Tote that barge, lift that bale,' as the old song had it. As an employee, you aim to use your time efficiently, knowing that others are observing and measuring your performance. In this world there is a strong focus on, and belief in, measurement — of output and of your effectiveness as an employee. Such measurement is seen as rational and objective, where judgement is old-fashioned and subjective.

After retirement, you no longer need to measure your success, and your performance is no longer judged. You can allocate your time as you wish on pursuits that cross the spectrum from frivolous to serious, not caring too much about efficiency and measurement.

Here's a practical example: learning a foreign language.

You could approach the challenge by studying, doing the tests, sitting the exams and getting the certificates: all good. But, and this is a *critical* difference, you could also simply work independently on improving your proficiency, slowly immersing yourself in the language and its associated culture. You won't be able to measure your success (other than by your ability to use your new language skills), but that's okay, as you can form your own judgement. Your stress levels will also be much reduced because you are not being measured.

This is a radical shift, because you have moved from being measured by others to judging your own success.

This is all about setting your expectations. The choice is yours. One of the great advantages of post-work, over when you answered to a boss, is that you can set your own expectations and work within those – you can even change them when you want to, without needing to ask anyone's permission.

There is another aspect to all this. Thinking of your career, how was your success recognised and even rewarded? Perhaps you received a promotion, a new job title, a pay rise, a bonus, or maybe just a compliment or pat on the back.

In retirement, most of these kinds of affirmation simply don't happen. You may struggle in the absence of such clear and tangible validation. But there is always an answer. If you engage in voluntary work, for example, it's likely that those you have helped will reward you with their appreciation. Or you may enlarge your circle of friends, who expressly recognise your support and friendship. Or you may simply enjoy the dawning of each new day and the possibilities it brings you.

## Teenagers and retirement

Who remembers being a teenager? Or at least being the parent of a teenager? And how those years were punctuated by parental rants and lectures, and banging on doors: 'Tidy your room!' 'Do the chores we agreed on!' 'When are you going to start studying? You have an exam this week!' 'Get a job!'

We remember our teenagers' inertia, yet, while nothing seemed to be happening, it was in fact a hugely productive time for them in which they gathered strengths and life skills. Time has a different meaning for teenagers, who imagine a long life stretching out towards a distant horizon.

With retirement, life's timeline begins to close in on you. If you retire at sixty, statistically, you have twenty-plus years ahead of you, which means the clock is ticking.

We know how quickly time can pass, so is this really the time to mope idly around the house? Why not get proactive, seek outside help, and develop a plan for these years?

## Risk and fear

Conventional wisdom has it that risk aversion increases with age. It sounds reasonable, but let's look a little deeper.

First, think of financial risk. In retirement, where there is no prospect of gaining income to top up your retirement account balance, it is natural to become less tolerant of investment risk.

Second, sadly, physical injuries take longer to heal as we grow older, which may understandably discourage older people from skateboarding or mountain biking. Not only that, but our reflexes and reaction times slow, which is more reason for caution. Besides, falling on your backside becomes less elegant (and more demeaning) the older we get. It's that status thing.

Moving into retirement, we need to be aware of SAHS, or Stay at Home Syndrome. Even though there are sound reasons for becoming more risk averse as we age, this is a trap to avoid. We need to keep experimenting and seeking personal meaning. To experiment requires that we take risks — measured perhaps, but risks nonetheless.

Think of the analogy of a house on a cold winter's day. Outside it's cold and hostile; inside it's warm and comforting. Some retirees fear stepping outside the house. Perhaps subconsciously, they fear the change from comfort to challenge. Despite all its difficulties, their work life had an element of predictability that made them feel safe. They got up at the same time, travelled to the same place, worked with the same people on the same tasks, and went home each evening for rest and recreation.

Outside the house of these retirees in their sixties, there stretches a golden path. They won't have that many years ahead for a healthy and productive life. Maybe ten or twenty, possibly thirty years? So why not get out there and make the best of those years and take that golden path. Yes, it's uncertain, but it will surely bring many unexpected rewards.

## Reflection activities

- Check your diary for the next month: Is it too empty, too full or does it strike a good balance?
- Do you have your own room in your house or apartment, and what do its furnishings say about you?
- If you have a partner, have you had serious retirement discussions together?

# MEANING: WHAT IS YOUR PURPOSE IN LIFE FROM HERE?

*'From my personal experience, I want people to know that the first period of retirement is not straightforward. Think of it as a change of climate in your life. Even if you are prepared for it, you will have to adjust, to call on your own resources and those of others.' (Marg)*

Now we've completed the preliminaries, let's roll up our sleeves and turn to the essence of retirement coaching and how it can help you to generate a fulfilling life post-work.

## Regret: The hidden emotion

What is regret? According to the dictionary, it is a feeling of sorrow associated with something you did or didn't do, or didn't complete. Let's first examine the regret that may result from something you did. Perhaps it is over a loss that could have been avoided or an action that might be at least partially redeemed through the salve of a sincere apology.

In the financial context, the investment world is awash with regret. As any regular investor knows, things don't always work out as they should. A stock is purchased based on an expectation that a certain price level will be reached over a given time. When that outcome is confounded, the personal recriminations begin: *Why did I make the investment at that time? Look how well other investors have performed. I should have paid more attention and squeezed out a better return. I should have held onto the stock for longer to get a better price.* Investors don't always exercise the discipline of a fixed exit point, and even if they do, they may still regret selling a rising stock too early.

Another source of regret is over things not done or left incomplete. Older people commonly reflect wistfully on the deep past: life partners chosen or not chosen; career choices made; a job transfer offered and rejected; other opportunities spurned. It can all seem so much simpler and clearer in retrospect. 'If only I had …'

There's something really interesting about this type of regret, and very useful for retirees who have the luxury of time they lacked during their career.

Australian palliative care nurse Bronnie Ware spent several years with terminally ill patients in the final weeks of their lives. In 2011 she wrote a book (described as 'part memoir, part inspirational guide') entitled *The Top Five Regrets of the Dying: A Life Transformed by the Dearly Departing*.

The most common regrets of the dying, uncovered from her conversations with patients, might be paraphrased as follows:

- **I lacked the courage to live a life true to myself** (rather than doing what others expected of me).

- **I spent too much time at work** (and missed out on so many other things life offered).
- **I lacked the courage to express my feelings** (settling instead for a detached and colourless relationship with the world).
- **I lost touch with my friends** (realising too late the cost of failing to develop and nurture friendships).
- **I should have been happier** (seeing too late how happiness is a choice that old patterns and habits can deny us).

Now you have time and opportunity, you *can* do something about these regrets of inaction. If, for example, you regret that you stopped playing the violin when you were eleven, then take it up again. If you never travelled to the destinations you wanted to, now you can.

When reflecting on your regrets, choose to make positive changes now. Of course, it's not always easy to sit and work with your failures, but by learning from past mistakes you can build a better understanding of how to address and reduce these regrets in the years to come.

Don't berate yourself with regret over the choices you didn't make or the paths you didn't follow. To state the obvious, making a choice to do something will always mean choosing *not* to do something else. So rather than stress about it, try something new now.

Rather than dwelling on regrets, viewing retirement as a blank canvas gives you the freedom to try to move forward and experiment with different choices.

## The importance of friends in retirement

Think about how a traveller from Venus might regard our approach to retirement on planet Earth. The Venusian might be concerned to observe such an abrupt discontinuity in the life of retired Earthlings, who move from being productive workers one day to unemployed seniors the next; they might also note how little training they receive on how to deal with this transition.

Let's address our Venusian's concern by talking about how Earthlings can build and maintain friendships in retirement.

So let's think about friendship in the context of work and retirement, duty and pleasure. Why so? Well, when you worked, you probably found that the balance of duty versus pleasure could sometimes load in favour of duty. It could at times become quite a troublesome and fraught negotiation with self and others.

The reason that this negotiation is difficult during your working life is that time is then such a restricted commodity. It is generally much easier in retired life, when time constraints loosen, and it becomes possible to choose the balance between duty and pleasure. You may decide to work for a charity or to look after grandchildren, both of which can build a sense of commitment or duty. But you may equally decide to lighten up on duty and give more time to pleasure, and this is where friends can be so important.

Now you can spend as much time as you wish with your friends, especially if they too are retired, unlike when you were time poor and had to juggle competing commitments. And having a strong network of friends in retirement can go a long way to compensating for losing the high level of social interaction you had in the workplace.

Cicero had some good advice to share on this topic. As a Roman philosopher and statesman, Cicero thought and (luckily for us) wrote a lot about friendship. He rejected the idea that friendship required an equality of goodwill, demanding some sort of balance of debits and credits. A person should not be concerned that giving more to a friend than you receive in return is giving out more to the friend than is their due.

Friendship, he argued, should have no truck with insincerity or hypocrisy. In fact, flattery is a mortal enemy of friendship. Flatterers say everything with a view to pleasure, and nothing with a view to truth. Advice between friends should be given freely and openly but without harshness, and should be received with patience and without resentment.

While acknowledging the value of seriousness and gravity, Cicero believed friendship should be unrestrained, genial and agreeable. This brings us to an extremely serious topic, loneliness, which is the flipside of friendship.

A dearth of friends will frequently lead to loneliness, a condition that may arise at any stage of life, but is particularly common in later life.

In the ever-connected world of social media, you may feel, and appear to others to be, surrounded by friends when in fact you are not. On the surface, you may feel socially engaged and busy as you bounce messages and posts back and forth on Facebook, Twitter and Instagram, but this may not satisfy a need for genuine connection, which can best be found in real-world community and connectedness, with friends and family, or through clubs and classes.

Think of individual time versus community time. Time on your own in superficial busyness versus time shared with others. The quality and quantity of those connections will be a highly personal consideration. How many people you would feel comfortable sharing your deepest feelings with is a question only you can answer.

There's no pill you can take to cure loneliness. And the simple prescription of getting out of the house to find companions to share activities with will work for some, but not for others. But sociability, service and companionship (whether with a life partner or a casual friend you meet with at a café) are all useful remedies.

## Values and value

As a worker you were valued by, and delivered value to, your employer, your clients and others.

Now, if you are retired (or about to be), let's generalise this and look at three related concepts of value that will be extremely personal to you. How important is it to you to feel valued, to know that others think that you are valuable to them? And are you offering this value in a way that is consistent with your own most important values?

Practically speaking, you may want to sit in your garage making model boats strictly for personal pleasure. That will have value for you. It is said that traditional Chinese artists would create a work — say, a painting or pen sketch on paper — then roll up the scroll and never show it to anyone else.

At the other end of the spectrum, suppose you decide to volunteer for a charity working with sick people. Almost certainly you will feel your contribution is valuable to others and will feel valued by them, in a feedback loop. And doubtless you are connecting to one of your own deepest values — that of helping others less fortunate than you.

In summary, we can think of these as the 3 Vs — to give value, to be valued and to connect to your values. To do this you should:

- **Clarify** to yourself and others what you want to achieve.
- **Connect** with others of like mind.
- **Celebrate** these three values that you now enjoy.

Is this so different from the satisfactions you experienced when you worked?

Let's bring to the fore three questions for retirees or those about to retire (who are swinging on the gate between work and post-work):

- Do you want to feel valued?
- Do you want others to think that you are valuable to them?
- Are you living in a way that is consistent with your own most important values?

Now is the time to discuss implementation.

It should begin with the discovery of your most important personal values. Obvious values that are central for many people (although not all) are the drive to give to others and the drive to obtain greater knowledge.

In brief, values connect to your beliefs, and you not only tend to hold these beliefs with emotional force, they can often drive your behaviour. For the creation of meaning in life, they are the garden where the retirement coach can help you to grow your answers to the other two Vs: giving value and feeling valued.

## What lies beneath

In everyone's life there is a hidden pattern that lies at a deeper level than the simple milestones of birth, education, work, retirement. This pattern – you might call it your authentic self – isn't always easy to distinguish, and may emerge only after deep reflection and long conversation.

We have all met people whose overt lives mask a hidden dimension. Think of the class clown whose laughter hides a deep unhappiness, or the person whose serial relationships disguise their search for a more meaningful partnership. What might those depths reveal in a person contemplating retirement?

Resilience and adaptability are two ideas that come to mind.

How well have you coped with change in your life? Have you bounced back from adversity? Have you been open to change? How you answer these questions will reveal a lot about your deeper, hidden self. If you answered yes to the last question, this will give you clues as to what options may open up to you in retirement. For example, activities that might work for you in retirement include study and travel — putting yourself out there to see how you adapt and develop.

If, on the other hand, your answer was no — and that's fine — then you might prefer to cultivate your garden, to paraphrase the last line of Voltaire's novel *Candide*, remembering that the gardening phase came at a point in Candide's life that followed lots of excitement and adventure. There will be many other responses and possibilities in retirement.

## Rhythm in retirement

Boredom and distraction are counterweights. If distraction here means not properly concentrating on a task, then boredom means settling into a 'non-task'.

In the workplace, distraction impedes you from doing the work assigned to you. That is considered a bad thing, almost as bad as being bored. In retirement, however, where work productivity is no longer the day's driver, distraction may seem a natural way to feel connected, to get outside of yourself.

There is another way to think about the relationship between boredom and distraction. If boredom occurs when the needle of your personal compass spins aimlessly, then distraction may be a useful way to reduce any anxiety that you feel.

As a strategy, however, distraction has its limits. If you can find a rhythm in what you are doing, then settling into that rhythm, you will no longer be distracted. This is also called flow.

Take as an example of flow reading a book for a period of time without being tempted to connect to the buzz of the world. But you don't have to be too hard on yourself. There's nothing wrong with breaking this rhythm after an hour or so in order to rejoin the wing-flapping of the distracting world for a while. Equally you could put the book down, do nothing, and pass into a state of boredom. We have more to say on this in the next section.

In the end, the balance will be a very personal one, to which no general formula for success can be applied. So experiment with a mix of boredom, distraction and flow. These three winds can gust and swirl quite differently for you throughout the day.

## Boredom

When children get bored, they turn to their parents to solve the problem, which can make parents impatient. 'Find something to do!' may be their exasperated response. This raises two questions: What is boredom? And what is to be done about it?

It's not easy to find a good definition of the term, but it does possess two general dimensions, which we can express as *the environment* (such as the boredom of a student in a classroom where an uninteresting subject is being taught on a hot day) and *personal motivation* (such as the boredom of an adult who can't get motivated to start certain activities). There is a complicated link at play between the environment and the desires of the individual. Either you are trapped inside the shell of boredom or you crack through it and escape.

In retirement, small doses of boredom should not create problems. If it persists, you may need to consider both your environment and your motivation — that is to say, your meaning or purpose now you have stopped working.

Possible remedies are to vary your daily routine and see what interesting and unexpected outcomes may emerge, and to reflect on past aspirations that you might want to revive.

Boredom is not your enemy. Indeed, it may be the spark that motivates you to find purpose and meaning.

## Utopia

Where is Utopia? It turns out to be nowhere at all, a 'no place' imagined by Sir Thomas More as a thought experiment in socialism. Utopia may be an imaginary place, but it has played and can still play an important part in our collective imagination. It's a device by which we can dream of and aspire to a better world.

History yields many examples of the idea. For example, in the mediaeval imagination, Cockaigne was a land of idleness and luxury. It was a notion that resonated in a world of narrowly concentrated wealth, mass poverty and feudal enslavement. The 20th century has seen many examples of political dictatorships rationalised by a utopian belief in a better world. As far as I can tell, they have all ended in failure and mass murder. But let's move to a more pleasant topic.

What could a retirement utopia look like? According to the marketing imagery, it would be a world of perfect sunsets, a loving partner and free-flowing alcohol — all in a beachside setting. Interesting, yes, but doesn't it more conjure up a short holiday than a long life in retirement?

To imagine your perfect retirement, you will need to dream your own dreams. Go to a quiet place and give your imagination free rein. Is it all about spending good times with friends and family? Moving to the country? 'Giving back to society', that idea you always thought about but never acted on? Only you can find the answer, although a retirement coach can help.

Dreaming about retirement, you may come up with something amazing. Sadly, life won't always live up to your ideal. So now take out the pruning shears and clip the branches of your dream into a realistic shape for your future. Good luck.

## Problem, cause, remedy

You have a toothache — perhaps you have a cavity or have lost a filling. So you visit the dentist — who fills the tooth and, after extracting some discomfort and money from you, the problem is solved.

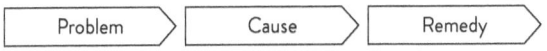

This sequence is more or less how each of us engages with the professional service provider, whether doctor, dentist, solicitor, tax accountant or financial planner.

After a lifetime of work, a new retiree sits at home wondering what to do. Travel, grandkids, charity, golf, charity, golf. The list continues. Now, suppose this wondering turns to anxiety, to arguments with their partner, disputes with their children, a lot of engagement with the internet to no purpose. This could turn into a problem.

Following the flowchart above, a problem has a cause, right? What is the cause here? In many cases, it's a lack of meaning in the retiree's life, or at least the kind of clear-cut meaning it had when they worked.

And what is the remedy, you ask? We say it's to engage with a retirement coach. Of course we would say that.

So it all comes back to your personal search for meaning. Once you have found it, you can make the most of those early years of retirement while you have the health, mobility and motivation for it.

## Money and you

In *As You Like It*, Shakespeare proposed 'the seven ages of man'. In relation to money, we suggest just three: teenager, mature adult and retiree.

A teenager's attitude to money is generally fairly simple: It comes mainly from Mum and Dad. In later life, with its complex mix of financial aspirations and burdens, the mature adult's thinking will turn to future needs, which may include debt reduction, saving for retirement, thoughts about a financial legacy and many other considerations. The retiree may be thinking primarily about security through the years of radically diminished earnings, or no earnings at all.

As we pass through these three phases of life, our attitude to money continues to change. In a simplified way, we might think of these changes as they relate, in varying proportions, to three *S* words:

- **Security:** How much will I need to retire on?
- **Spending:** Do I enhance or restrain my expenses?
- **Status:** Is the amount of money I have important to the world?

The challenge for *all* of us is to rethink our attitude to money as we move into retirement, being carefully aware of the risk that we may be applying an outdated model of what money means to us. It is legitimate to ask yourself at the point of retirement: am I operating off the correct emotional model for how I think about my money, or do I need to refresh it?

Three essential questions to consider are:

- How much time do I have at my disposal?
- How much money do I have?
- How much energy do I have?

Our thinking, at different times of our lives, might be depicted in the following matrix:

| Age | Time | Money | Energy |
|---|---|---|---|
| 20 | ✓ | ✗ | ✓ |
| 40 | ✗ | ✓ | ✓ |
| 60 | ✓ | ✓ | ✗ |

A successful retirement for you may depend in part on the extent to which you can turn that final ✗ into a ✓.

Let's get practical. Money is relevant to retirement. We can't deny it. By the time you retire, you will probably have a financial plan in place. One way to think about your financial plan is to assess your AAA Rating.

Your AAA Rating depends on how *you* answer this question: Is your Annual income Adequate for your Aspirations? Simply stated, is your annual cash flow from your various assets sufficient to support the life you want to lead in retirement?

## Renaissance art and retirement

What is the image of the practising artist today? Probably that of a solitary creator in a studio. It wasn't always like this. Many great Italian artists learned their craft through apprenticing in a studio with other artists under the charge of a master painter.

With their contributions of a leg here, an eyebrow there, they were not so different from many modern workers who work in teams to learn and practise their trade. Beyond this, modern workers often belong to an informal social club at work. Here they can test personal ideas and share knowledge with colleagues, perhaps on no more than where they might take their next holiday or the name of a good builder.

These kinds of connections can be lost after you have retired. So where can you find such networks through which to test your thinking, learn new ideas and continue to grow after you cease working?

There is no single answer, of course, and much will depend on the individual. It may be a golf club or a men's shed;

it may be through connecting via the internet with very different people from distant parts of the world to learn about other cultures and languages.

A coach can be a useful guide in helping you to find answers, but in the end the choice is yours. You are also an artist, a creator of the self.

## REFLECTION ACTIVITIES

- Have you lived with a regret that you can now take action on?
- Have you made any new friends recently?
- Are you absorbed in your devices (iPhone, tablet, computer) more than you need to be?

# MASTERY:
# WHAT ARE YOUR GOALS IN RETIREMENT AND HOW WILL YOU MOVE PURPOSEFULLY TOWARDS THEM?

> *'Everybody's different, but I think a crucial element is to have something that interests you, that can occupy you, and give you some satisfaction. And I think you've got to have something to look forward to.' (Bruce)*

It's all well and good to work out your meaning in life post-work, but what are the practical steps to build a pathway towards achieving them? We call that mastery.

In the retirement context, mastery might be understood as 'possessing the skills and knowledge you need to maintain control over what goes on in your life'. Research in Australia by Donaldson, Earl and Muratore (2010) showed that mastery significantly predicts retirement adjustment, and that feelings of mastery correlate positively with wellbeing.

In a separate study, Osborne (2012) found that approximately one-third of retirees have poor adjustment styles in retirement, observing in particular that when people retire they usually take their existing personality traits, attitudes and behaviours with them. The author argues that this increases the likelihood of significant shocks and losses upon entering retirement.

The research points to the need for retirees, and soon-to-be retirees, to build an awareness of the adjustment process they are undergoing.

Now that you have done the work to extract your personal meaning in your post-work life, it's time to take it to the next level. Your meaning may extend in directions that are unclear and unpredictable at the outset, but you now need to consider setting a timetable. A typical issue is to think about the support as well as the obstacles that you may encounter. To put it simply: *I want to achieve X. What are the practical steps I can take to do so?*

## The portfolio lifestyle

It is almost commonplace to talk about a portfolio approach to life after full-time work, rather as if it were a collection of separate activities that are meaningful to you. Let's look at some general principles you can apply that could help you to clarify the components of your own portfolio of retirement activities:

- Define your purpose and your meaning in life post-work: You can always change it over time.

- Build your social network: You had one at work but now that's gone, so you need to replace it.

- Develop yourself: This is personal, and your ideas for yourself may not suit others.

- Have fun: You can now; and best of all, the boss isn't watching.

How does a portfolio lifestyle look in practice? It is unique to the individual, and that is its magic. Also bear in mind that you can be as busy as you choose to be.

## Framing

*'For there is nothing either good or bad,
but thinking makes it so.'*

**HAMLET**

Think of yourself looking through a window at the world outside. The window frames a small piece of the world for you to admire. But it's only a small piece, not the entire world, and you know that.

This concept of framing has many more abstract applications. A beef marketer will promote a product as ninety per cent lean or ten per cent fat and find out which frame is more compelling to consumers. Is your glass half full or half empty? Your answer may reveal something of whether you see the world through an optimistic or pessimistic frame.

In retirement, you can frame your outcomes. In your world of work, you probably thought you were time poor; in retirement, you find you have acres of free time, and this will set you free.

Free to do what exactly? Free to experiment and take up activities and a lifestyle that give you pleasure. That has to be good.

## Predicting the future: Writing and telling stories

In 1898 an American writer Morgan Robertson wrote a work of fiction called *Futility*, (later published as *The Wreck of the Titan)*. The *Titan* was a large ocean liner, and its fate prefigured that of the famous *Titanic*, which sank fourteen years later, in many uncanny ways:

- Both did not have enough lifeboats.
- Both sank in the North Atlantic.
- Both fatally struck an iceberg one night in April.
- Both ships had been described as 'unsinkable'.

Let's settle on this as a series of improbable coincidences, though Robertson himself referred to his 'extensive knowledge of shipbuilding and maritime trends'. What has any of this to do with retirement? Please stay with us as we develop an analogy, but this time as a story with a happy ending.

To pose it as a question: Are you able to 'write the book' of your retirement feeling that you can pretty much predict a good outcome for yourself? In other words, by thinking about the opportunities and risks that may or will present themselves post-work, can you figure out your own solutions to what comes next in your life?

## Becoming a child again

A strange thing can happen in later life, whether on the threshold or inside the temple of retirement. Assuming that at least one of your parents is still alive, you can become a child again. What does this mean?

To explain, once upon a time, many years ago, you left home in order to grow up. Perhaps you travelled, became preoccupied by work, raised a family. You may have done all of those things and more. It's likely that over those many decades, your relationship with your parents changed — from child-to-parent to adult-to-adult.

Now, though, if your parents are old and frail and you are not, you may settle into an old routine. You are their child again, but with a stark reversal. They will have emotional demands on you. They will want your help, and suddenly you have the time to give it to them.

You may want to think about this, discuss it with friends and others in the same phase of life, and meditate on what it means for you. Planning and anticipating problems can be a very useful approach to becoming a child again; after all, it has never happened to you before.

## Lifelong learning

Because we have all passed through some form of education in our lives (school, technical college, university, for example), we tend to think of learning as a bounded, finite activity. Attend a course, study, pass an exam: That's it. But now, in retirement, something magical can take place. It is called lifelong learning. What do we mean here? It is the open-ended engagement with a subject or subjects where, certainly, learning takes place, but in an unpressured and more joyous way. Moreover, you can choose: woodwork, Latin, Flemish art. The list goes forever.

The main characteristics of lifelong learning are that it is flexible, self-motivated and ongoing. There are many benefits for people in retirement. For example, it builds social networks and can increase involvement in voluntary activities. Larger social networks and voluntary work are both associated with improved mental health. Better health and increased social participation can mean reduced healthcare costs and a greater individual contribution to the community.

> Lifelong learning encourages creativity and resilience in people. This increases their ability to:
> - Manage uncertainty.
> - Communicate with others and build relationships.
> - Improve their conflict resolution skills.

## Mona Lisa and retirement

The *Mona Lisa*, surely the most celebrated painting in the world, was stolen from the Louvre in Paris in 1911, but returned three years later. There is a story around who committed the crime and his motivation, but let's look at why this is the most famous painting in the world today.

It wasn't always so famous, and it didn't always hang in the Louvre. It is received wisdom that its creator, Leonardo da Vinci, was a genius. He was also an obsessively dedicated worker. While we can check off these twin ingredients for success – skill and hard work – the notoriety surrounding the theft of the painting also played a part in creating an aura around it that survives to this day.

In terms of its growing fame, we could call this the Mona Lisa luck factor. By this account, success relies on three factors: skill, hard work and luck. We prefer not to attribute our successes to good luck (although we may blame bad luck when things don't go well) as it disturbs the narrative of self we create, but luck usually plays a role, for good or ill. That is, luck can be a positive or a negative factor.

On the positive side, you can create good outcomes that come from luck by:

- Expanding your network of connections.
- Being curious and aware of possibilities that may be good for you.
- Experimenting and taking risks.

Who knows, you may meet interesting people, find new meaning in your life and have altogether more fun too.

But remember to pace yourself — you are no longer working.

## Phases of retirement

Retirement need not consist of a single, undifferentiated block of experience. Was your work life uniformly monotone? Of course not; you shape-shifted through many tasks, jobs, perhaps even careers. You know how, during your working life, a new phase of work was either imposed on you from above or planned for.

We have noted before the importance of those first few years post-work, when you are brimming over with plans, energy and good health.

Now, consider the possibility of phase two. This may happen after about five years, when you are ready for new challenges. Our advice is that you start to plan phase two before it comes knocking on your door. Quite simply — say, at year four — review and evaluate what you have achieved so far, then start to dream about future possibilities. Don't have phase two drop on you out of the blue. Plan for it.

## Your legacy in retirement

Legacy is a concept with two senses. The narrow definition relates to a bequest, perhaps an inheritance, passed down from one generation to the next. But legacy also has a second, related meaning.

Each of us leaves a trace in the world, sometimes by accident. If by design, then it is something we think about and plan for.

If you are already retired, your work legacy is effectively sealed in a box, a box that when opened may release fair or foul odours, but once you've ceased employment, there's not a whole lot of useful work you can do on that legacy.

Now you are retired, you can think about your legacy (your trace in the world) in at least two different ways.

First, you can ponder the ways in which you can help other people, perhaps through charity work, devotion to family or simple friendship. You now have the time and space to work on this, if you choose.

The second kind of legacy is subtly different from the first. It's the things you achieve for yourself — perhaps selfishly, perhaps altruistically — that define the way in which people will remember you: She was a good golfer or pianist; he was a fine cook and was always so friendly.

Now, the sense of legacy is getting quite diffuse when compared with a specific financial endowment.

In your professional life, you may have worked in a role that everyone understood, or at least thought they did (you were a bus driver or a doctor, a carpenter or a teacher), or you were someone whose precise role remained something of a mystery to most people.

But all that's in the past. Now, in post-work, do you feel that other people understand what you are about? Perhaps you don't know yourself, and perhaps that is a problem for you.

The answer tends to arrive more easily once you are clear on your meaning and purpose in retirement.

A trace in the world is what you leave behind you. It's all about how other people perceive you, a mystery we may wrestle with our whole lives. As the Scottish poet Robert Burns once expressed it, 'Oh would some power the gift give us, to see ourselves as others see us.'

## The Retirement Game:
## A framework to help you understand the dynamics of any couple post-work

Do you remember playing Snakes and Ladders as a child? Here is a version for adults who are dealing with the whole retirement thing. The players of this version are a husband (let's call him Jack) and his wife (Lily), both in their sixties. Jack has built a career over forty years, while Lily built and sold a successful business before retiring a couple of years ago. Jack has recently retired and wants to join Lily in all her pursuits — charity work, mentoring, golf, movies and so on. She already does these things, but with her own friends and connections — and without Jack. She is determined to keep it that way.

If playing this game with your partner reveals issues that you can't resolve, then perhaps 'Jack' would benefit from seeing a retirement coach.

**START PLAYING: ROLL THE DIE.**

| Community garden | Fishing charter | Return to work | Photography class | **HAPPY RETIREMENT!** |
|---|---|---|---|---|
| Fund-raising | Neglect friendships | Learn Mandarin | Meditate | UK driving holiday |
| African safari | Volunteer at local hospital | 10km Fun Run | Swim the Cole Classic | See the Northern Lights |
| European river cruise | WA campervan holiday | Start a business | Teach primary school ethics class | Learn an instrument |
| Lack of exercise | Walk the Inca Trail | Health crisis | Charity work | Rotary Club |
| Trekking in Bhutan | Write a book | Enrol in art class | Toast-masters | NZ South Island driving holiday |
| START | Join book club | Act as a mentor | Take up yoga | Join Park Run |

## REFLECTION ACTIVITIES

- Think about your legacy, and be open to revising your thinking and plans.

- Do you have a desire to learn a new skill or take up a new activity?

- Do you conceive of your retired life as having several phases?

# REAL PEOPLE, REAL STORIES: LEARNING FROM TALES OF RETIREMENT TRANSITION

*'I would have liked some assistance in working my way through the emotional battlefield of retirement – where do I find my meaning and purpose when I am no longer teaching? How do I create a satisfying new structure for my days? How do I find motivation and courage to try new things?' (Jenny)*

An example is worth a thousand theories, and there is much you can learn from the retirement experiences of others. The insights, wisdom and experiences of those who have embarked on their own retirement journey can serve as a useful guide for anyone beginning to visualise and plan their transition to the next phase of their life.

The purpose of these case studies is :

- To share examples of the types of triumphs and challenges people face as they experience the retirement transition.

- To allow you to tap into the wisdom and experience of those who have already retired.

- To explore the problems individuals and couples face in making a successful retirement transition, on which an external perspective can be very valuable.

- To give you inspiration and ideas about activities that may be of interest to you as you design your own retirement.

---

# CASE STUDY OF THE 4M PROCESS IN ACTION

Philip (not his real name) presented himself, at what was to become our regular coffee shop for the six sessions, as a man in his late sixties with some current health issues. In a natural way, these formed a part of our continuing conversations. He is a man who is easy to relate to and who talks freely about himself while staying on topic. He considers that he is mapping out his retired future over a five-year period, which for him sounded reasonable. This formed the basis of our engagement.

He has two adult children, both living remotely from him, and is married for the second time, and happily so. He intends to fully retire this year. As happens in these sessions, apart from the waiters serving coffee, the conversations of other patrons were merely background noise that never disturbed our focused concentration.

As I walked him through the 4M process over our six sessions, I learned more about his background and his aspirations.

The first M covers what he will miss from work. He is clear that he won't miss the stress — this is a matter we will return to later — but he will miss the mental stimulation of work.

The second M involves a cognitive assessment of how he currently spends his time, given that he is already semi-retired. Here we uncovered an interesting expression: He admitted that when not in the company of his wife, he 'bumbles along'. This is not to say that it is necessarily a negative, but it needs addressing as he moves into full retirement and grasps its full meaning.

The essence of the 4M process is the third M, meaning, and it was here that the most productive work occurred. He is clearly a man with many interests and activities, and he intends to develop these further in retirement. Interestingly, he declared a couple of 'wild card' interests that may take some courage to fulfil but certainly fit into the category of outrageous ideas for him to pursue. In terms of mainstream activities, in the near term, he first cited an upcoming move out of the city. Then he stated an interest in 'voluntourism', being a combination of committing to voluntary work and doing so by travelling outside Australia.

He seems to have a robust circle of friends, which should serve him well in the future. When reflecting on the retirement experience of friends, he saw *grey nomad* and *grandparenting* as the sum of their activities.

The final M is very much a wrap-up of the previous one, in which we discussed practical steps for some of the activities that he may pursue. Included was the importance of his investigating some of these in the here and now, and at the same time thinking through any help and/or hindrance he may encounter in their implementation.

As I got to know him better, we analysed (not in any great depth) his tendency towards catastrophising events and circumstances in his life. Using the diagram below, we began with the aspects of his life that he felt he could control, an example being the type of work he has done for decades. Now many things in life were uncertain but, as I explained to him, what he needed to do was to prevent those from sliding into a catastrophising frame, from his point of view.

I suggested that he practise taking matters out of the third box, holding them up to the light for rational examination, then try to measure, understand, evaluate and even mitigate their consequences, in order to move them leftwards in the diagram below to reduce stress levels. Given his analytical background, this idea appealed to him.

| Locus of control | Uncertainty | Catastrophe |

> The six sessions were beneficial to Philip as they were an opportunity for him to reflect on his future as he moves into retirement, by allowing him to take responsibility for creating a list of activities that will bring joy and fulfilment in his new stage of life. That is the essence of retirement coaching.

## Robyn and Paul: Living outside their comfort zone

Paul, sixty-two, is on stage giving a speech at his local Toastmasters club on the role radio has played in his life over the years — both as a listener and more recently as a presenter.

He recalls that during his career driving government vehicles for the Nambucca Shire Council, the soundtrack to his days was talkback radio. For years, his pet peeve was that he wasn't in control of the radio station in the truck he shared with a co-worker, and he especially lamented having to listen to John Laws day after day.

'Then I got promoted, got my own truck and could listen to Richard Fidler on the ABC,' he says.

He recounts the story of how, after he retired, he became a community radio presenter (an activity he says pushed him well beyond his comfort zone). He had grown weary of the country and western music played on his local station, so he and wife Robyn, a former bank manager, did some training and launched their own community radio show.

'We went into radio because we both love music. There's so much great music out there, and I wanted to play it. It also leads us to take holidays that involve music festivals, and that's very enjoyable,' Paul says.

No two retirement transitions are the same. Some people plan their gradual exit from the workforce meticulously, then ease effortlessly into the next phase of life, while others have retirement thrust upon them. In their late fifties, Robyn and Paul found themselves in jobs they were struggling with, and they decided that if the numbers stacked up, they were both ready to retire.

Robyn says, 'We weren't planning to retire when we did, but we were in jobs we were really not enjoying anymore. I think both of us would have kept working if we were happy in our work, but it was sort of forced on to us. I always thought I'd like to retire when I was around fifty-eight. I nearly made it — I missed it by a couple of months — and we were just thankful we were in a position that we could finish up.'

These days, when not helping out with grandkids, their retirement diary includes golf, fishing, gardening and camping, which represent a continuation of hobbies and interests they had enjoyed throughout their working life.

At the same time, Robyn and Paul have broadened their horizons and pursued a creative new direction far removed from their careers in local government and banking. After dabbling in some short courses in computing, poetry and creative writing at the University of the Third Age, it was public speaking and community radio that would become their passions in retirement.

Robyn says, 'It's an exploration stage in life. I think you've got your basic interests that you've always had, and then there are the new activities that come up by surprise.'

These new pursuits offer an outlet for them to explore their creativity, while providing valuable social connections and a form of routine in the absence of paid work.

'Toastmasters turned up and that got us into a timetable, so between that and the radio show there's something we go and do every week.'

While many retirees find it useful to maintain structure and routine in their lives, the challenge is to keep busy enough without restricting yourself. In the rush to fill your schedule in retirement, Robyn suggests it is easy to end up with more commitments than you can handle.

'We've become a bit entrenched in the week-to-week things, instead of getting away and doing more travel, so we've lost a bit of freedom. It's a very fine balancing act. You want to give back through the things you're involved in and to do a good job, but then you feel a bit guilty saying you now want to take off for a couple of months. But I think we've got to the stage this year that we're going to have to, because otherwise we'll never get away!'

While Robyn embraced her creative side and threw herself into a lot of new activities, the reality of retirement was very different from her expectations.

'It was a steep learning curve. What you think you're going to do and what you *actually* do in retirement can be very different — like the radio show we do. And then Toastmasters is even more outside our comfort zone,' she says.

Such talents and passions can lay dormant throughout a career, only to awaken in retirement when you have the time and energy to explore new paths.

More than once during our discussion, Robyn refers to the need for 'balance' in retirement. She advises others who are contemplating finishing work to try to find the right mix of leisure activities for their own enjoyment, spending time with family and learning new things for themselves.

As with most couples, they've inevitably needed to make adjustments now they are spending forty extra hours per week together. For couples, forging a new identity in retirement is about striking the right balance between individual and joint activities.

'As much as we like doing things together, it's also nice to have a bit of space, and to maintain your own friendships,' Robyn says.

Both admit that whatever is going on for you psychologically, the retirement experience can magnify those emotions.

Robyn and Paul found value in gaining an external perspective on how to make the transition easier. Such input and guidance may come from a retirement coach or a counsellor, who can offer new ways of thinking about an old problem.

'I'd highly recommend that, because if you suddenly find you're spending 24/7 with your partner it can magnify little problems. A big thing for us was communication, talking about what activities you will be doing and where you're going to spend your money.'

Robyn and Paul's advice in a nutshell to soon-to-be-retirees:

'When I was working,' offers Robyn, 'I thought as soon as I finished I would travel overseas for two or three months. And I know a lot of people do that. They finish up one week then go on a big holiday, and I don't think that's a good idea. You're better to ease into things.' Paul agrees: 'Don't try to do too much. Let your body rest and get over the working life. Transition into retirement at your own pace.'

## Catherine: Tuning in to the rhythm of retirement

While the first year of retirement is often eagerly anticipated, life doesn't always follow the script, and for Catherine (a lover of music and singing), getting into the rhythm of retirement has taken more effort than expected. In fact, the first eighteen months were anything but a harmonious experience.

After a career as an English teacher followed by a several years in curriculum development and teacher education and support, Catherine began her gradual transition to retirement at age sixty-one.

'I truly loved my career as a teacher. There were highs and lows, but I really loved classroom life and I loved schools (and I still enjoy any opportunity to be in a school). However, I think I was getting a little tired and jaded. There seemed to be no time for anything but work. I think you can stay too long and it's best to move on before you become stale.'

She began to reduce her hours in the education department where she worked, and at the end of 2011 she set up a small educational consultancy. Her aim was to work more flexibly in the educational arena, supporting teachers and passing on her knowledge and experience. At the same time, Catherine wanted to develop her interests, and, most importantly, to spend more time with family.

Between 2012 and 2016, Catherine worked in many schools on a sessional basis, and also worked part-time for a non-profit organisation tackling issues regarding teacher training and leadership, and educational disadvantage. While busy with her ventures, she had more time for family, and particularly her two young granddaughters.

By the end of 2016, Catherine was ready to wind down and retire permanently. 'I was about to turn sixty-six and the joys of retirement beckoned!'

At the beginning of 2017, she and her husband moved from Canberra to the Southern Highlands, to be closer to family in Sydney. The experience of selling, buying and moving after nearly thirty years in Canberra was stressful, but the thought of retirement and its pleasures was exciting. However, the first eighteen months of retirement were not ideal and held some big challenges, as Catherine explains:

'We moved into the house, which needed significant and immediate work, in February. In April I had knee replacement surgery, and was out of action for several weeks. This coincided with a very dear friend of forty-five years (more like a sister, really) becoming very ill with liver disease. Visiting her was distressing as it became apparent that she wouldn't recover and she died in February 2018. This happened a week after my two-year-old granddaughter had open-heart surgery. I felt so much emotion as my granddaughter lay in one hospital, being treated brilliantly by a surgeon and medical staff, and with a positive prognosis, and my darling friend lay dying in a palliative care ward in another hospital.'

Then, just a few months later, Catherine's son, who lives in England, went through a traumatic marriage breakdown and she went to stay with him and support him.

'So, it was a tough start to retirement, I think made harder because of being in a new place and not knowing people. But in some ways (and hoping I don't sound Pollyanna-ish), if these situations were going to happen, the timing was fortunate, because I had retired and I had space to manage all these things. I didn't have to worry anymore about work commitments. So I was very grateful for that.'

Now into the third year of retirement, life has settled down. Catherine realised that to feel at home in a new place, she had to 'get out there, and meet people'. She became involved in many activities, including choir, book club, table tennis, voluntary work, folk dancing, exploring the Southern Highlands and travel. She also has time to exercise more and is taking greater care of her health and well-being. She has joined the University of the Third Age (U3A), which she describes as 'an absolutely marvellous organisation, offering a huge number of courses and interest groups to members'. Catherine recently agreed to join the U3A Southern Highlands' committee as a way of contributing to the organisation.

Catherine has also reflected on some of the other hard issues about retirement.

'Although the Southern Highlands are very beautiful, we missed Canberra, our friends there, the familiarity of the city and our previous activities. So, there was, and perhaps still is, a period of adjustment.'

Another persistent thought for Catherine was to do with identifying her meaning in life. 'Am I now just a narcissist enjoying the good life? Where's my meaning? What should I be doing with my time? At times I've felt a level of depression, or perhaps guilt, about this stage of life.'

Despite such moments of uncertainty and ambivalence, Catherine is very aware that retirement offers the gift of time to pursue interests and to keep learning. Like most retirees, she is very busy. She is especially glad to be closer to family and enjoys regular contact with them. Family members come and stay with her and her husband, and she experiences joy in being closely involved with her granddaughters.

'Gradually I've come to see that my meaning in life is very much anchored in people,' she says. 'Whether it's time with family, catching up with old friends or coffee with a new friend, or the book club, I enjoy being with people, listening to them, encouraging them, sharing stories and laughs, supporting them where there is a need. It's not a career with all the kudos that can come from those working years, but investing in others has enabled me to begin to settle more contentedly into this stage of life.'

Catherine's advice for soon-to-be-retirees?

'In the years leading up to retirement, I think it's important to develop some interests, and it's really important to be kind to yourself, because retirement is unsettling, and it can be perplexing. Some volunteer work is great, and is an important way of continuing to contribute to the community. But it is also important to make sure you and your family, or you and your partner, are on the same page about how retirement is going to work for each of you.

While I felt ready for much more recreation and fun times, my husband still wanted to work, albeit on a sessional basis, and wasn't as ready for total retirement. We're still at that stage and allowing for each other's perspectives, timing and activities.'

So, what does the retirement dream look like now?

'I want to continue to sing, dance, walk, garden, talk and share, drink good coffee, care about and support others, enjoy the arts, attend concerts, play table tennis, read more books, stay as healthy as possible and travel. And then there's revisiting learning French and piano playing. Oh, and I think I'll join a ukulele group.'

## Marg: Pathway to an exciting new phase of life

While retirement is often thought about as an event at a point in time, it is becoming increasingly common for this chapter of life to play out as a colourful transition over many years. The idea of a 'phased retirement' can be appealing as it involves making a gradual transition from the intensity of full-time work to a more flexible, less taxing set of activities. Where possible, phased retirement allows you to remain involved in activities that are meaningful to you, while easing into retirement in a timeframe of your choosing.

After a varied corporate career spanning over twenty years and covering many different roles – from Sales to Human

Resources, Organisational Development and Learning – Marg retired from corporate life in her late fifties. During the course of her career, which culminated in her role as Vice President of Human Resources and Organisational Development at an ASX Top 100 Company, Marg developed a deep knowledge of human behaviour, with a particular interest in leadership development.

After calling time on her career as a senior executive, Marg pursued a portfolio of activities that allowed her to leverage her skills and corporate experience, on her terms. She was mindful of incorporating a degree of flexibility in her schedule – a welcome change from the rigours of sixty-hour weeks as part of a leadership team reporting directly to the CEO.

Marg embarked on this new phase of life by pursuing postgraduate study. After a brief period of rest and relaxation, she returned to university to gain a Master's in Organisational Coaching at the University of Sydney.

'Returning to study after thirty-plus years was a little daunting, but I relished the challenge and thoroughly enjoyed learning and making new friends,' Marg says.

Combined with her corporate experience, the study inspired Marg to launch her own coaching and leadership consultancy. She also found time to join a number of boards of not-for-profit entities — all in the first year post-work. Marg felt she still had a lot to offer people trying to reach their full potential and still really enjoyed engaging in corporate life as a consultant rather than an employee.

Marg has always had a deep commitment to giving back to the community and she has worked in a voluntary capacity for a number of organisations, mainly through board roles, but through hands-on volunteering too.

She says, 'It's satisfying being able to contribute to a charity's success and seeing positive results. There's so much wonderful volunteering that can be done. Once you work out what it is you are really interested in, you will find something, because there is just heaps out there.'

One such charity is a not-for-profit organisation aiming to improve the employability of women in need by providing, free of charge, professional clothing, a network of support and the career development tools to help women achieve self-sufficiency.

This organisation supports women in need from a range of backgrounds. From supplying outfits for court appearances for women in correctional centres, to working closely with women who are unemployed and struggling to find work for a host of reasons. In these cases, the charity helps by providing suitable clothing, advice on CV preparation, and workshops on interview skills, to boost the chances the women will secure a job, often after a significant period out of the workforce.

Marg says, 'It's all designed to wrap as much support as possible around these women.'

Marg enjoys the variety of her schedule, and while she has no plans to retire from her current activities, she sees herself 'in transition' and has considered the topic of retirement from many angles. Her advice to others contemplating the next phase of life post-work?

'From my personal experience, I want people to know that the first period of retirement is not straightforward. Think of it as a change of climate in your life. Even if you are prepared for it, you will have to adjust, to call on your own resources and those of others. However, I found you will soon transition to an exciting new phase of your life.'

## Jenny: Retirement is a time for re-invention

In a career spanning more than thirty years, Jenny was a high school English teacher and assistant principal at schools in Sydney, Perth and Canberra. She loved her work, and never really wanted to retire for the simple reason that she couldn't imagine life without teaching. The prospect of a world without her colleagues, who were also close friends, and without the young people she enjoyed teaching and nurturing, was not an appealing one. Jenny felt she had nothing to replace those things.

'I loved my work,' she says. 'It was, for me, a vocation rather than a job. Retirement was about being old and alone; I didn't want to go there. It did take me a few years, and a life-threatening illness, to understand that I could re-invent myself. I am at last becoming the person I have wanted to be. And I am happy.'

After retiring earlier than expected in her fifties due to family caring commitments, Jenny found the early period of retirement challenging. The transition from the highly social environment of teaching to the relative uncertainty of the next phase of life was hard to manage.

'I would have liked some assistance in working my way through the emotional battlefield of retirement – where do I find my meaning and purpose when I am no longer teaching? How do I create a satisfying new structure for my days? How do I find motivation and courage to try new things?'

Several years later, following her recovery from ovarian cancer, fortunately caught early, Jenny was given the gift of a new appreciation of life and a strong desire to be all that she felt she could be, to herself and others. She decided to try new things she hadn't thought of doing before, to see what might be possible. At seventy, never having run previously, she trained and completed her first half marathon through the streets of Sydney.

Jenny says, 'That gave me the confidence, the following year, to do some trekking. My glutes had made it very clear that the brief window for running was now closed!'

The following year, Jenny trekked the Inca Trail in Peru with a group for Ovarian Cancer Australia, and together they raised over $30,000. The Everest Base Camp trek in Nepal was her next mission. Jenny trained with younger people who would often say they hoped they would be enjoying similar adventures when they were in their seventies. She describes the Everest trek as the hardest yet most rewarding challenge she has undertaken.

'I loved every minute – from the exhilaration of reaching Base Camp to the breathlessness and aching legs on arduous daily climbs. The camaraderie with amazing, young and not so young people on these adventure challenges is simply awesome. And there is little to compare with walking in the heightened awareness of the Andes and Himalayas: breathtaking scenery, a sense of one's place in the soul-stirring beauty of nature: We are small but we are not insignificant; we can be magnificent.'

Jenny feels fortunate to be able to travel overseas. She followed her Everest adventure with a two-week trip with a friend to Rajasthan – her first visit to India. No physical challenges here, but instead Jenny describes a wonderful assault on the senses:

'Colours, spices, car horns and the "language of the road",' she says. 'All around were silk fabrics, smiling faces, extreme poverty and wealth side by side, religious ceremonies, Diwali lights, music and dancing in the street, fortresses and rural life. Beautiful people. I come home from these experiences so enriched by the people and culture I've encountered, and I remain in contact with many via Facebook and Instagram. My world of friends has grown!'

This year, at age seventy-two, Jenny is joining a friend on the 790-kilometre Spanish Camino Walk over forty days from St Jean Pierre de Pont to Santiago. She describes it as another physical challenge of endurance to keep the body strong, while providing a 'personal and spiritual challenge'.

'I also want to focus on being a good grandparent to my eight gorgeous grandchildren and hopefully inspiring them to live full, happy, confident lives.'

## Bruce: Embracing a passion for art

Artist Bruce's father was an accountant with a passion for numbers and helping people. So much so that he was still processing tax returns for a small number of clients at age ninety — just two weeks before he passed away. Bruce chose a different retirement pathway from his father, finishing up in his role as a senior manager for a major national retailer at fifty-five, and relocating from Sydney's northern beaches to the picturesque surrounds of Berry, on the New South Wales south coast.

The relocation was driven by Bruce's desire to get away from the pressures of business in order to focus on his passion for art. Prior to his career in the retail industry, Bruce worked in advertising and attended a number of prestigious Sydney art schools. As he reflects on this earlier stage of his life, and association with subsequent Archibald Prize winner John Olsen, we conclude that Bruce's time as an artist in the sixties might best be described as his 'creative period'. Many years later, he felt he now had the opportunity to indulge his creative side and revisit his love of painting.

'Here was the dream: Retire right on fifty-five and change my career. I wasn't thinking of it as putting my feet up and reading the newspaper. I had an intense interest and desire to become a more skilled artist — a craftsman — and the idea of becoming a master painter appealed to me. So it was a matter of changing my occupation, but to one that I was not necessarily financially tied to. So [I had] the idea of coming to the coast and setting up a studio, because I have the artistic ability — I never lost that.'

Bruce and his wife Patricia built their new home at Berry and included a purpose-built artist's studio. After spending the first couple of years studying art books, and attending classes run by a local artist, Bruce began painting and exhibiting. He decided to combine a love of travel with his art, and during holidays in Italy and France, Bruce would take photos of picturesque villages, cafés and scenic landscapes as inspiration for the paintings that would later feature in his exhibitions.

'I was always looking for the real world, and the old villages... the back canals of Venice where, you know, real-world people obviously live. I'm looking through the camera and visualising a painting. I got a lot of material from that and we brought it back, and I did a series of paintings on Paris and Venice, and themed my exhibitions around those subjects.'

Bruce has gone on to hold exhibitions of still life paintings, seascapes and marine works, and he is currently painting a series of pieces for an abstract exhibition. I ask him what it feels like to painstakingly produce a series of paintings for exhibition and then to be judged on that work.

'It's really rewarding. I've had a lot of exhibitions, I've been there, and I've had tremendous feedback. I think selling art is like selling houses. You've got to find just the right buyer who loves it,' he says.

Bruce's retirement transition was well planned and methodically timed, so I am not surprised he has some well-formed views on the prerequisites of a fulfilling retirement.

'I think primarily you need to be occupied and to do something you enjoy doing,' he says. 'It's a major stage of your life. Your life is your work for a long period of time and I think a lot of people fall into a vacuum when they retire and say, "What am I going to do with myself?" Maybe I was lucky because I had some talent in an area that was not related to my work, but I think everybody's got something. And if you can find something that really interests you... it might be studying law, it might be making wooden tables, it might be painting, or doing something with your hands. Everybody's different, but I think a crucial element is to have something that interests you, that can occupy you, and give you some satisfaction. And I think you've got to have something to look forward to.'

Indeed, in the commentary we read about the inputs to happiness as we age, 'having something to look forward to' is commonly mentioned. Bruce lights up as he articulates the activity that puts a spring in his step each day.

He says, 'You know, I'm halfway through a painting... I can't wait to get up tomorrow morning and get back on it, get in front of that easel and start slapping some paint around. You know, it's really great. That's what makes me tick.'

## Jon Glass: Transition to retirement coaching

After a thirty-plus-year career as a leader and senior executive in the investment industry, Jon was ready for a new chapter, but he wasn't ready to retire. Jon has a PhD in Pure Mathematics from Cambridge University. He was also the Chief Investment Officer of Media Super, among other senior leadership positions in Australia.

Rather than retire to a life of leisure — and after doing some specific training — Jon established a retirement coaching consultancy, 64 PLUS (www.64plus.com.au), to share his experience and insights in order to help others make a more successful transition from their working years to the next stage of their lives.

'As reiterated in this book, while there is a tremendous amount of focus on preparing financially for life after work, many simply do not give the same level of attention to the non-financial preparation needed to achieve personal fulfilment,' he says.

The longer you live, Jon believes, the more carefully you need to think about how you spend those extra years to maximise your health and wellbeing, and achieve a meaningful life. He says the definition of 'meaning' will differ for everyone, but the research suggests there are some common activities that improve the probability that you will find happiness beyond the working years.

Jon points out that the demand for retirement coaching is increasing for two reasons.

'Firstly, executive coaching has been popular in the workplace for a while, though not a long time. Secondly, the baby boomers represent a large cohort of retirees — the largest we have seen in this country.'

Jon works with his clients to explore some of the major questions that will confront you when you decide to transition to life beyond your career, regardless of what form it may take. What is truly important? How would I like this phase of life to unfold? What are the goals and objectives that matter to me and my family? What is my purpose in life and am I living in alignment with that purpose?

For example, what combination of casual or part-time work might appeal? What hobbies might you pursue? What community activities could you participate in? What are your travel priorities?

Jon believes the job of the coach is to listen carefully to these individual expressions to get to the heart of the matter — which, put simply, is to locate your meaning in life post-work.

Jon encourages clients to think creatively about the life-changing transition they are embarking on.

'For example, in many cases, a person may never have worked for themselves, having always worked for others. So, one definition of retirement is that you become your own boss and employee. Are you going to be a kind boss?' he says.

Jon is, of course, a strong advocate of retirement coaching services. But before you engage a retirement coach, he believes you must first begin a dialogue with yourself and with the people who are most important to you.

'Ideally, these matters should first be considered long before retirement — say, in your mid-fifties. Many people do this with their finances, and that's good. But it seems that in our society most people have yet to grasp the nettle when it comes to planning for their emotional future. It's time to start that dialogue with family members and friends. Test their reactions. After all, retirement isn't a single isolated event — it's an important phase of your life.'

# CONCLUSION

*'We don't grow old. When we cease to grow, we become old.'*

**RALPH WALDO EMERSON**

Where to from here?

Let's recap the critical concept from the introduction. The things your job (or business) provides that you may miss when you retire:

| | |
|---|---|
| **MEANING & PURPOSE** | You could easily define your purpose as a worker |
| **ROUTINE** | You knew where you would be every Monday at 9am |
| **IDENTITY** | You had a job title and you felt you were needed |
| **ACHIEVEMENT** | You finished a successful project and felt good |
| **SOCIAL CONNECTION** | You had work colleagues you could relate to |
| **VALIDATION** | Your boss told you how good you were (sometimes) |
| **SATISFACTION & PLEASURE** | You completed a week of work and sat back and smiled |

We hope that reading this book has given you deeper insights into what this table means for YOU.

## Top tips to make your retirement transition a success

- Have a conversation with your family. Talk to them about your ideas. Listen to what they have to say. Don't surprise them two years later. It doesn't mean you have to spend hours and hours talking about it. Just sitting down and having a chat puts people at ease and gives them a sense of confidence.

- Think of ways to decouple from your work life. You've been working for the past forty or more years, so of course it's a large part of your life. Slowly transitioning away from work is not an easy process, and you can afford to be patient with yourself.

- Ask yourself, 'How busy do I want to be?' As your own boss, you can sit and watch the waves roll in two days a week if you want, or you can be on ten committees and eight charitable enterprises, and pick up your grandchildren from school. That's a choice only you can make. It's not one to make in perpetuity, but it's something to give some thought to.

## YOUR NEXT STEPS

When you worked, you were often pressed for time. Now, in retirement, time is an asset — we could say it's your best friend. Learn to enjoy this new relationship.

We have made frequent reference to retirement coaching and we strongly recommend you explore the idea of engaging a retirement coach.

Retirement coaching is an opportunity to reflect deeply on your path in life and your aspirations for the future. It is a short-term investment in the long-term wellbeing of you and your family. The decision rests with you.

# ABOUT THE AUTHORS

## JON GLASS, PhD

After I left full-time work in 2014, moving to part-time work, I spent a lot of time in my study pondering my future. Should I go back to a full-time job? Should I construct a portfolio of activities or simply take it easy?

The prevailing discussion about retirement then seemed to reflect some very negative feelings that I couldn't make sense of for myself. I would commonly hear the following questions:

- Is retirement bad for your mental and physical health?
- Does retirement keep us small and limit our possibilities?
- Is retirement always about slowing down and decline?

I soon rejected the idea of returning to full-time work. I felt that at age sixty-two I had done enough of that. However, I was determined to have some kind of significant employment, so I set about creating a retirement coaching practice called 64 PLUS. I had already studied counselling at the Australian College of Applied Psychology, and augmented that with study at the International Executive Coaching Academy.

I wanted my coaching practice to be part-time to leave space for other activities in my life, such as writing, teaching, music, languages, travelling and spending time with friends. I try to present to my clients an image of a man who, in his late sixties, remains active and engaged, in the hope that some of my enthusiasm will rub off on them. Here are some of my current activities:

- I run a retirement coaching consultancy (64 PLUS), helping individuals make more effective transitions to life after work.
- In 2018, I wrote and produced a play called *Entitled Transactions*, which was a sellout at Marrickville's Factory Theatre.
- I teach Primary Ethics classes at the local primary school.
- I am a self-published author of children's books.
- I am a keen student of foreign languages.

It took me some time to find my rhythm in retirement following a working life that required me to get to the office early each weekday. There the rhythm was constant — meetings, appointments, documents to write, clients to meet — often to the sound of the clock striking the hour.

Was the transition easy for me? No, it wasn't. I had to think and feel and experiment until I came up with a series of formulae that worked for me.

That last part is critical, since everyone is different. Without delving into the theory of personality types, let me pick on something very simple. I am a goal-oriented person by nature and always have been. On my bookshelf I never have just one book in play at any time, I have several — sometimes absurdly many. Some people would prefer to let the world unfold for them in its own time and not bother with setting goals. In some ways I envy them, but pointlessly, as I know that's not me.

Finally, some of the answers to the question of 'What is the meaning of my life in retirement?' may be delivered without the help of a 'midwife', but I'm certain that for many people the application of some skilful coaching will lead to a better outcome. Retirement coaches exist, and will multiply over time, to serve what I see as an emerging need in our society.

## DAVID KENNEDY

David is a retirement planning specialist and author of End of the Retirement Age – an upbeat commentary on the reinvention of retirement, featuring inspiring stories of older Australians from all walks of life. He has discussed retirement trends on ABC Radio Sydney, Sunrise, 3AW Radio Melbourne, and 6PR News Talk Perth. His views on retirement planning issues have appeared in The Sydney Morning Herald, and The Australian, and he is a regular contributor to Starts at 60.

David writes about the redefinition of retirement, and argues for the need to re-frame the conversation about the ageing population in positive terms, while placing greater value on the potential economic and social contribution of older Australians, who (on average), are healthier and living longer than at any point in history.

For many years, I have been fortunate enough to spend my days in conversation with countless people in their fifties, sixties, seventies, and beyond who are planning their retirement, or are already retired. In this privileged position, I have listened to the hopes, fears and dreams of a generation as they prepare to transition from one phase of life to the next.

In my retirement planning practice, I have focused on assisting clients with financial preparation to ensure their funds last the distance (seeking to replace a salary with passive income in retirement), but it is increasingly apparent that there is so much more to effective retirement planning than money.

In addition to a salary, the workplace provides many things that can be taken for granted – a sense of meaning and purpose, a source of routine, a forum for social connection, and a component of our identity. In order to thrive when you reach the end of your career, it pays to be mindful of how you will replace these things when work is no longer in the picture. In different ways, each is critical to our wellbeing at every stage of life.

How consciously and effectively you prepare for the retirement transition, in particular the first 12 months, may well determine the quality of your experience in the decades that follow.

# Hear from Jon's retirement coaching clients

*'Like a lot of new retirees, I thought I had things organised.
But I was thinking financially, not psychologically. It turned out,
as I'm sure it does for a lot of men, that I was totally unprepared for
the psychological changes brought about by retirement.
Jon's program really helped me deal with my change of lifestyle.
It provided a framework to help me understand why I was feeling the
way I did, and how to redefine and reorganise my life
to get on top of things.'*

*'Jon was very easy to talk with and very understanding. I found his
ability to direct me into maintaining focus and direction in my plans
and activities for a successful and enjoyable retirement extremely
helpful. He has definitely helped me to overcome my natural habit of
falling into the trap of procrastination. Thank you so much, Jon'*

*'Having had a strong involvement in retirement planning and financial
planning over many years, I thought I was reasonably well prepared for
retirement. However, Jon provided an extra dimension by broadening
my outlook on the way ahead — while at the same time personalising
strategies to be quite specific to my own circumstances.
A worthwhile program.'*

*'I had an absolutely necessary discussion with Jon that identified how little preparation, other than the obvious financial preparation I have really put into retirement planning.*
*Better to have several years to plan and prepare now than to discover the abyss the day following retirement.'*

*'I found the 4M process very clear and relevant to my needs.'*

*'I found the coaching process used by 64 PLUS easy to understand and very useful.'*

# SOURCES

ABS, Retirement and Retirement Intention, Australia, 2016–17.

Conley, Chip (2018), *Wisdom @ Work: The Making of a Modern Elder*. Currency.

Donaldson, T., Earl, J.K., & Muratore, A.M. (2010). 'Extending the integrated model of retirement adjustment: Incorporating mastery and retirement planning', *Journal of Vocational Behaviour* 77(2), 279–89.

Elliott, Herb, & Trengove, Alan (2018). *The Golden Mile: Herb Elliott's biography as told by Alan Trengove*. Runner's Tribe Books. Second edition.

Jefferis, Chris (2018). 'Unrequited obsession', *Sydney Morning Herald*, 11 October.

Jobling, Ian. Herb Elliott interviewed by Ian Jobling for the Sport Oral History Project (sound recording). https://nla.gov.au/nla.obj-221973309/listen

Lane, Daniel (2014). 'Herb Elliott motivated by pursuit of perfection not cash or glory', *Sydney Morning Herald*, 23 February.

Lee, Bruce Y. (2018). '11 Seconds: How long your doctor listens before interrupting you', *Forbes*, 22 July.

Osborne, J. (2012). 'Psychological Effects of the Transition to Retirement', *Canadian Journal of Counselling and Psychotherapy* 16(1), 45–58.

Plumb, Emma (2019). 'Modern Elder Chip Conley: Valuing seasoned workers both curious and wise', Respectful Exits, 19 March, https://www.respectfulexits.org/blog/modern-elder-chip-conley-valuing-seasoned-workers-both-curious-and-wise/

Robertson, Morgan (1898). *Futility*. M.F Mansfield, New York.

Rule, Billy (2016). 'Herb Elliott on how to succeed in life and sport', *Perth Now*, 13 August.

Turner, David (2017). *The Extreme Phronesis of Percy Cerutty: A Narrativized Life History of a Legendary Sports Coach*. University of Hertfordshire, Hatfield, UK.

Ware, Bronnie (2012). *The Top Five Regrets of the Dying: A Life Transformed by the Dearly Departing*. Hay House UK.

**CONTACT 64 PLUS AT**

Email: jon@64plus.com.au
Telephone: 0409 116 766
Web: www.64plus.com.au
Facebook: 64PLUS
LinkedIn: Jon Glass

**General advice warning and disclaimer**

David Kennedy is an Authorised Representative of Hillross Financial Services Limited (ABN 77 003 323 055, AFSL 232705). Any advice in this publication is general in nature and does not take into account your objectives, financial situation or needs. You should consider whether the advice is suitable for you and your personal circumstances and you should obtain professional advice where appropriate before making any such decision. Material in this publication is not intended to provide specific guidance for particular circumstances and it should not be relied on as the basis for any decision to take action or not take action on any matter which it covers. To the maximum extent permitted by law, the authors and publisher disclaim all responsibility and liability to any person, arising directly or indirectly from any person taking or not taking action based on the information in this publication.

www.ingramcontent.com/pod-product-compliance
Lightning Source LLC
Chambersburg PA
CBHW032043290426
44110CB00012B/929